I0236566

This book is dedicated to
 the working class. Although I mean the
 tradesmen/women of which I belong,
 I do include in that portion the very few artisans
 that when in rare form produce certain
 things such as these that pulsate in the veins of creativity.

Contents

Preface

Within the field of understanding there are infinite possibilities. Our struggle for knowledge within these understandings defines who we are as individuals. We build ourselves and destroy former selves amongst these realms. They are the blood of the human race. The limits given that hold us in mortality. As far as we have come and will go we will never grasp and fully comprehend these understandings. When we feel we have it and our fists hold it tight, it will again turn to liquid and ooze out between our fingers.

At the age of 31 I have a profound realization now, that I will never obtain a complete understanding. I do know that my removal and attempt to do so, to define, has led to a state of being which we all celebrate. I have removed all rights and wrongs, completely let go of worldly senses to the best of my ability, and removed any human measurements of time and space. And here I sit, sharing.

The preceding will lose you at times. You will be as I have from time to time. None of what you will read is a concoction of the imagination nor is it a mockery of an artistic mind. The words within are presented as a painter on a hillside formulating his view of the landscape. It is a letting go though, on every end of common human conception,   allowing you to give a song, a voice, color, to the quiet in a mutual intimate bond.

Images of Light, Somber, and Ethereal

There are no rights and there are no wrongs.
There is only love.
You will either choose to live in it or not.

From Light (for the Good lord)

When the shadows rose I was there
Awake
Many walks I had taken at that hour to find myself

I was troubled by previous understanding of a standard
A disturbing silence
A field of torture

When I turned gazing
Through something thicker than oil
It wasn't something emerged
Not happenstance

It was her
Light
Love
The woman
Forgotten
Rediscovered

How I remember now
Remember how the delicacy that
Held my calloused soul
My rugged spirit

Of this unrefined
Walking willingly
Through the darkness of beauty
Holding my hand

Touched as no one will ever be
From you
Me to you

What none of my vitality will ever be
Will be you through you though

When weak you will carry
On my last step you shall be

In your eyes my absence
My worn hand then on your body

Here
On a missing parchment
Which love was written
Found
Pieced
The perfect model
Sculpted as one

Endeavor

Exit yourself
Find what you really need to breathe
Inhale the day
Hold for the night

On dust at dawn
Proceed to.
Move.
Because once in motion...

As the world circles
Circles around
You
Us

The strangers find to comfort
Flies in fire
Resistance brings warmth
Pale, white, broken

Tethering and tied
On your path
To return
To life,
 Love divine.

This commonality
Makes us whole
You may stray
But last you lie engulfed
In its fabric

Hymnal

It is God that has given me body
Trusting that I will reach perfections
To work and be examples

I come from time to time in body
To fuel Good when evil rises

I still fail
I acknowledge
Learning

Innocence

Like the moth we are drawn to the light
We flutter and circle
Instinctively
Only to land in the flames and be born
Leaving behind the ashes of body

An immortal union
Eternal

Divine Reflections

I especially love those that feel me in the breeze and see me in the sun. That even in my vacancy I have presence. Love it is because I hear them in the morning trees and breathe them on humid shores.

They always believe there is something more, something greater than physical senses. Nations call them dreamers but religions call them saints, priests, and prophets.

They are teachers, the passive kind. That work in love and instruct through silent examples.

They are the builders of beyond because they serve. Providers they are like mirrors to the light. Divine reflections.

Into Spirit

Cold and repelling
Intriguing though
So much as to be drawn from the comfort
The warmth

Over again to the desk
Mediator to my thoughts
This page my canvass
Pen my brush
Medium to the soul

Silence?
Hardly
The me that gets seen by those who read.
Horror
Maybe terror
To me RAPTURE!

Screaming and soaring.
Riding flames
Fires of love
Ashes of death

Bouncing off auras:
Desperate needs of fame
Acceptance
Attention
Users of time and space

The push never slowing
Only deflecting
Damp palms as spirit leaves body

I covet their stillness at times
How simple
To be
Simple

I proceed to play though
In the openness
Where comforts of shelter are non-existent
Not lacking

This is where my spirit climbs
Not to heights
To where you are touched
By what they call silence

Qualms among the iridescence
Subtle
Calling
Infringing on stability

An offer only to those who seek
Who dare join the experience
Intimacy is shunning
Breaching reality
A perfect exhaustion of physicality

Where one never rests
Because there is no need
Infinite dwelling amongst the heavens
Existence only in this fury
Madness
Passion

Not quiet

Soul Rider

Dust between stones that cling to your skin like
Geological leeches
In summer's sun
Dampened garments on a highway afternoon breeze
Hair playing vulnerable to air torrents
A smell of chlorophyll glistening and rubber soles

If it was a fall endlessly then let it be

Songs bleed through neighborhoods
To my ears like coagulants
Burning oil melting tonsils
And the lisp of steam release
Diesel vomit and clouds of dust

If wings touch then forever act

Salvation

Your demons I'll carry
On my back
On leashes

Like they are mine
To the ends of forever
While they maul me

I smile knowing you're safe
Please forgive
Know I am real as I take them away

On skins
On wagons of death
I take them far from you
May I!
Rest in peace

Their wings cover me
But not my light
I love so I shine

Chains
Nooses
Crowns of thorns

No solid,
 My friend

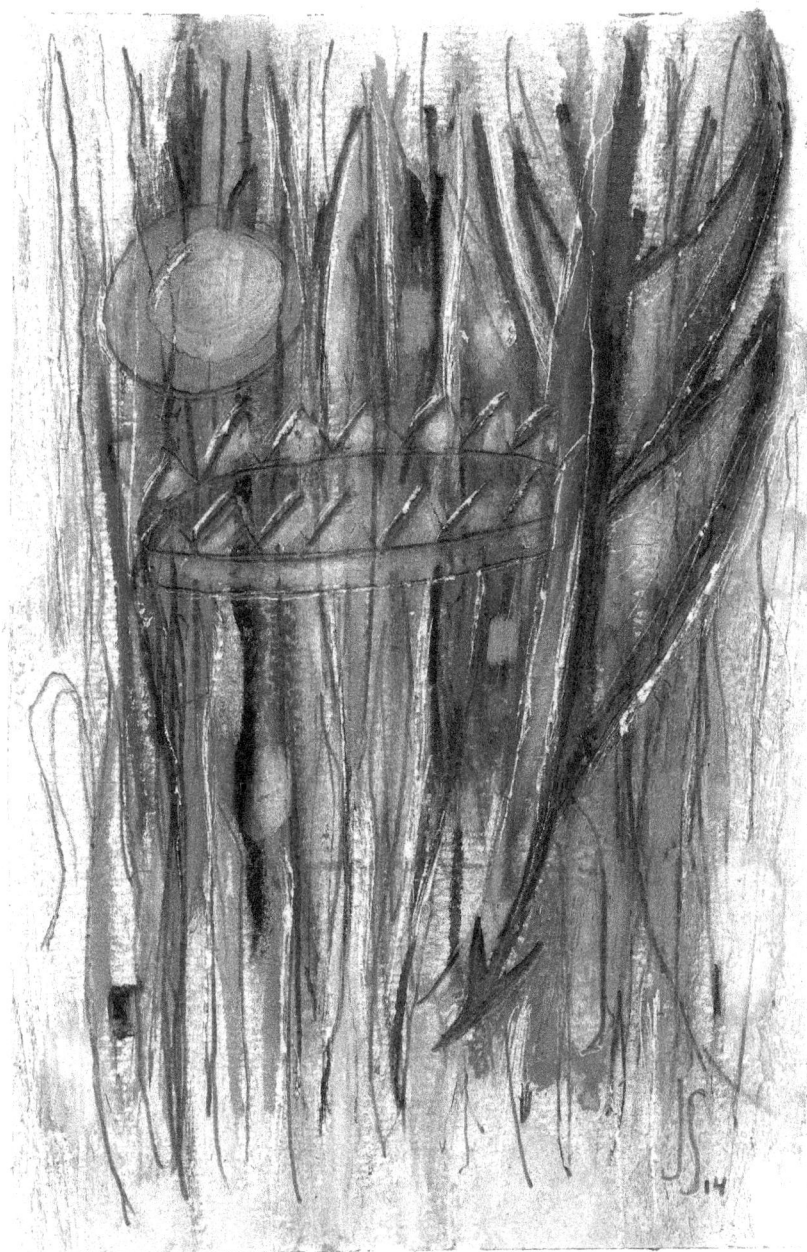

Champion

Wings drenched in wrong
Drying in the light
Pacing rows of tombs
The kind he cannot connect with

Isolated
Mortal seeds growing
Turning in rotation

He, blitzing the dregs upon leaving,
Ravaging
Then leaping in flight
Behind
Leaving impressions

On toward the ends
Distant and striking fear
A hunter
Adventurer
Solitary and comfortable

For the next arrow to come from his mouth
Piercing the next liar
Longing love
Because he comes open his spirit on his sleeve
Some fear
Within
Creating his own enemy

Spirit Guide

Time has perished
The moon goes down on the prophet
Beds full of skin fragments
And silk laden with intercourse

The city is even quiet
Marrow feeding hounds
The woman's breast as the solemn oasis
Youth in skirts shimmer to a fountain

Very soul sprained
Through the veins of conquest
Cooing at the mausoleum
Orchestrating the gates from dusk horizon
Prehistoric flowers lean in limbo

Eyes photographing peripheral shadows
A native weeps and one muddles subjects voodoo
Blue night strangles orange

The mist now
The mist
Molding figures

Legend

Left broken
The scramble to gather personal pieces
For better
Without worse

Distilled in comfort
That exit.
The one where your inside combusts.
Where you fly

No touch
But you feel
Boundless
On fire

As fast as light
Not limited.
Removed from time and space
Glory

In its divine
Through your achievements
On love
On moving

To soar among peaks of celestial
To dive through valleys
Laden in dust
Leaving impressions

Like tracks
The one the hunters never catch
They learn from though
As you become myth

Modern

Time in essence with lips of freedom
Sad sheltered many
Coerced to bleed

Fresh thought to inhale
Cold wind on withered lungs
The simplest
… left with instinct

All of this to the humbled
Not speakers of words
Creators of words

As to this they carry gifts,
Where we offer insight
Insight to the other, the most of what remain unspoken

Stretched is spirit
Beyond notice
Beyond understanding
Not beyond touch

Feel this touch not because you look for it
Because it is real
It is natural

Paralysis

Time as it is,
Vicious illusion
And its torrent web
Placing me

Stealthily; moth,
Upon the fabric

Picking the strands of a still world from its teeth
The revolutions behind a serpent eye

Vivo!
Pario!

Under a halo
Smiling queen as the light deafens
The call feels its way through the basket of hours

I turn the hands
From the cove of the sun
My skin crests;
Numb

Solitary

Burdened by self
Gentle strides
The field dry for harvest

Following your steps
To where I met your ghost
And only the shallow roots
Cried their green tears

Young birds sang warning
Child with no face
As a fountain colors garden

Just my wings
Alone
No breeze to carry

Pieces

Peace is
Bits
Heart torn apart

To individuals I give
Parts
Of me
Please receive

A bull portly
Nostrils on fire
Withering
Terrified

My thoughts dizzy
To the table
Fallen
I speak clearly
Sober
Clearly

In the distance a woman
In red
In vain
Covered in masks of flowers

Dismal
The scene of a cell
No tone
Bare bones
The effigy of life

At times barren
Which
Heightens
Senses
Spirits
Heavy motives
For vortexual encounters

Fastened tightly
Surrounding
Riveted
Potential lasts

Reawake
I've said
My heart in pieces
Take me
Please
Instead

No Sleep for Soldiers

A vision
Without sight
Insight

(But what of love?
Discover
Uncover the past)

Bleeding is my spirit
From the blade of a foul beast
My wrists
Throat tight
The neck
Asphyxiation
Brass to my brain

Tired and weary
A breath for a second wind
My armor
Less chinks
Worn like the day it was made

Perched
Poised
Exhausted
My being
But awake
No sleep for soldiers

Vigilant to His ways
A mercenary
Ready
No fear to walk through the shadows
No sleep
For soldiers

Cataclysm

Looking west
Again
For the time

Raised by sinister earth
Cloud cover
Their knowledge with an anecdote
Cleansing

Body
A saturation created by parasites
This is where bones will lie
Unfortunate

Shadows
A Maverick
No dust
March
In the soil

Feeding off
Infecting themselves
Infections of themselves

Melody in the distant
Like a prayer
Pleasure not far from reach

Held down and bound
The never ending striving
For this is sought
Until a catastrophic climax

To decimate
Is not to put an end
This end infinite

Nostalgia

I've seen carriages
In black and gray venues
Drifting fast past yellow buildings
Passengers tucked casually away

Street corners full of music as tombs existed with the living souls
Dried and something hung from strings
Jars of grease and voodoo orphans

Candles linger final flickers
Streams of silk climb toward the ceiling flowing like servants walk
Sirens break silence

Falling rain now audibles on outdoor porches
Praying for lightning and being let down by mother's effects
If it is then
Fuck it
Show me the moon

Climbing on knees through the damp grass
Searching for patches of mud to cushion
Tasting rain water on asphalt and rubber tires

A cloudy morning
Still blankets
Covered in love
Saps from alpines

Tracing musical notes in mind
Blonde hairs in the cracks of the walls
So full of leftovers

Shaded Hue

Mother?
Father!
Morning

The gentle roll through the window
A glacier's feather hand
It weeps with love across my shoulders.

Sun, you weave the trees
            … first thing.
With your golden reeds
And hem your blades on
The garden floor

Do you wish we, if I called you Golden,
Could meet like strangers?
There, where I forget to sleep
Those poppy dreams
How you would forget me

My wrists I give to your
Delicate hands
Healing tongue
As the wind gets jealous
Acting and seeing her lover
In the audience
Smiling, laughing, with her best friend
She gives her most intense performance

Where time for the aging tree
And sparrow are one
From their beaks they sing orange
And spices
The ground hums your vision.
Under your wheel

A Look from the Outside

Bronze and the oak
Stale songs and green silver
Mirror where plenum echoes dance of portly handles
Of an iron spear

Laughter in gray
Rose-colored cheery noses
Perched on communal vows
In their rookery of forgotten demons

The suits of men pressed in folds
Collecting dust of tiny jubilant tears
To the tune of slender eyes
Fragile arms and women skin making love to the atmosphere

An array of casino carnival games
Spectating bellies guarding a spirit; models
Down it's dark runway

The illusory hour arrives
Retiring thoughts of the day
And the room empties like a pitcher of inebriated time-parasites
Relief in its verve of silence

Beyond the door
The poet sits
Nestled under falling sky
Giving inanimate golden tongue
Liaison of broken

Shadow

Oh shadow!
Where are you leading me?

I remember you as an infant,
so vulnerable in life's hour.
You walked with me.

But now …
Now you have become a warrior
With your blade in hand
Demanding I follow

It was you that pulled the petals from the moon
And threw its anther behind the clouds

So that you could impregnate the night!?
So your children could swallow the hills

Running from the morning

Like Dust

Laid out in the ancient of
pre-autumn
The wind's chisel
Picking the grains of me
And casting me down its blue ribbon
To forgotten fortifications

Where damp leaves hang to dry among
Tree foundations
The places where some cold blooded hides
And takes the humid in through its skin

Over looking down and landing on a mountain side village sill
To dry with clay pots
Clinging to rugs on the line
Tumbling to the tea cups watermark
Leaf of an oak table

No abrasion the world leaves
For I do not resist
I just let it have me

In the shade
Where my closed eyes reside
Letting sound of the soils color dance through my ear
Nectar goes craved

And the thorns of my throat flower a tired rose

The Plunge

So thoroughly over coarse plains and the chipped tooth of the forest her
lips murmur
While two little friends like messengers send kisses as honeybees drawn
to pollen breaths
A heavenly rhythm with snares of the moon's tongue
They parade in quiet corners as the scolded child of winged figures

Every murmur becomes a whisper
Love as wind passes from her lips into his heart like hummingbird hover;
piercing, penetrating
Palpitating thrones of earth from violent quivers in a fury of them en-
twined

Fires shine bright blinding vision eyes burning
Fingers become scalded romantic blisters from touch from taste
Bleeding out into swimming hole lives
Drowning as the winds changed and tide carries their throats to whirl-
pools of salt depths
Smoldering eruptions that make time theirs
And the world falls into place
Soft, gentle, fistfuls of essence

Vision

Toes of the night ran through me
As dead women covered me in the white silk of the moon

In the bones below their eyes sat a cherub
With wings full of sulfur

I cried to the broken branch of the beech and
From my mouth two roses grew
Taking flight, searching for the queens of midnight's scowl

The creek's pallet craved for the digested remnants of leeches
Stirred from its bottoms and the clay balconies
Overlooking the dried reeds

On the horizon a golden flock of feathers
Pulled with it deafening orange
The melody and footsteps of Christ
I felt the lamb put its neck on the earth's perspiration
And my eyes became arrows

Transient

What is it in her eyes that turn stone to dust?
What music does her hair sing?
And where do they stare?

I know that she wants
Chasing something but she calls it waiting
Being
Balance

Always something more
Others faults
A song
She's been here before
With a man who wasn't
In a field of fantasy trees
She planted

So we will sing her song that quiet song
And let her dream the tune
Of her demands

She calls pure

And they leave
In the forest of
Forgotten

His wings come
And go

House of Whispers

Yellow pebbles
Buds like poison
Tracks like fire

Into a wall we walk
Apparitions
The night falls
Shadows dance to the moon

Sinking in sand
Whispering to the wind
Knocking inside walls
Scratching not to exit

Feel a tug?
See that child carry the silk
Enter and close the curtain
The doors still open behind

There is no howling
The sea speaks like white noise
The bark on the tree cuts the breeze
A broken branch sifts the brook

We manifest until the glow of the sun breaks the horizon
Mockingbirds we are then
Barking at the dust

Nocturnal Emission

Those eyes were stars
Late night strobes
As the rose kissed stratus pulled in the midnight blues

Fingers to lips to pull wind
At the side of effervescent time mangles
A cascade in glass two lovers fell

The river sat silent and spoke awe
As women sat watching
Scolding their flowers
Mending damp lace

Spirits strung out rippling eddies
Current flowing from their mouths
Breast fed lambs shivered from light electric warm

It was a dance
An orchestration of movements
That fed the mother's womb

Birthed was the night

The Colors of Love and Colors of Death

We write about love like we should be bound in padded rooms

Macarism (for Madeline my daughter)

Velvet tongue.
Bitter roots.
Maple groves.
Summer's anthem.
The sky falls,
   Red & yellow

Bleached sands.
Silver serpent.
Withered wind.
Ivory moon.
The sky falls,
   Brown & gray

Backwater stale.
Quartz dove.
Folded fawn.
Whispering bark.
The sky falls,
   Green & blue.

Black … black…
   Black & white.

The child dances and plays

Play!

Green Ambience

Why ask?
Just be
The bird
Stationary but full of love
A tree.

Must it be known?
My bite not vicious.
A lover
A fighter
To be free

Set aside from paragraphs
Pages
Color
Where can she be?
To embrace
to give
All of me

Across the river
In the warm
Wanting love
Waiting
Frost attached to comfort

A stare into a pale dim
Sky
Lost alone
Begging to lay a finger in her palm

To play
Her hair
Golden as the light that brought us forth
To touch her warm fair skin

To the desolate sometimes
On return a new foundation
Cover her in all of me
I am

Never know just what had been carried
Crying
For not this way then surely without hope
Surely her wisdom
Never knowing
Her a piece of me.

Ardent

If I didn't have eyes maybe my heart wouldn't spiral
In other lives we've danced
And here, this chance, we reach for something more
Distractions that make me weary
Delusion and I need discipline

I am not afraid to die.

Starve I would
Stand in flames
Weighted I would jump in the depths of the sea
As if fear could not touch me

It is love that gives me courage
Understanding and focus
I could cease comfortably

True

Lay.
With me.
A thousand times,
Then forever.

Mutual Whole

I have called you poetess in everlasting lives
An answer sung silent eyes
Our gathering a Senate
Manifestations of time's echoes and virtuous divine teachings
My conveyance of memories, prior learning
You scribe
Emergence to things forgotten

As the earth's children, deep in wonder, open arms in love
Embracing each other once again
Wars are wiped clean
Saviors are reborn
Becoming everything

Our gaze comforting
Pleasant reminders of coming

23 Enigma

Our souls collide ultra-nova.
The beginning of our universe
Silent space, glimmer of distant stars
I've seen your eyes, they hold love of angels
Mine like energy exerted over pent up time
As we looked and touched fusion we fell
Vulnerable, falling, but the darkness
Couldn't bind what could not
be caged.
Nuclear, omitting light, we slice open the
darkness.
Sending rays toward distant galaxies

We've embraced too long.
What brought us together is now the same thing
that has torn us apart.
As your light faded, I did my best to not let go.
You scorched the hand that would
have never put you down.

Falling away

I believe seeing some kind
of smile.
Was it because I gazed upon other stars?
Now that I lie in this system
One distant body that circles me
Never ending
Reminding
You are still out
there.

Psalm

Speak so cleverly
Our words of silence

Exhale:
my inhale
Eyes giving psalms

In my palm
Your cheeks
Fingers in your hair
Gently over your ears

Lips touching
Angelic love

And our breath was lost

Deluge

It is again
Kiss in the rain
Touching
Gentle
Drops on intimacy

Softly sod pushing
Souls
Our feet
Elevating us in spring

Cleanse
Birthing blossoms
Crocus perching
Love like perennials

Tasting nature
Perspiration
Seeping
Wash on facial terrains

The tumble now
Seeds sprouting
On our cheeks
Pasted in earth

Penetrate

Another breath from your energy
Your eyes like pillars of polished granite
Your mouth a flower
Dispensing opiatic pollen, inebriating my soul
Lips like that of sweet fruit exhausting your love

I shall not wait another minute
I shall not waste one either
An hour with you last for eternity
As you lay your stones
I fill the voids following

I would play with you in the subarctic that is space
Our fire I know will keep me whole

On last, on last like womb if it spills
Shavings
Fall back to me
Madly
Insane
Like our first encounter
Like we do when we cycle
When we are fury

Caress the buttons on your chest
Those that hold your skin back
Impenetrable
Like cast iron to my fingers
I kiss your heart
Because those before me have scarred it

Two Canes

I want to uncover your skin like
Wild roses
Your breasts; thorns through my hands
Rolling thunder through scarlet hills

Taste you like Mediterranean wine
In the brisk morning from
Barren balconies
Your thighs like beds of clover valleys
Singing from the sun, songs;
Honey in my tea.

How I would love for the chime
Of your smile
That makes trees dance in yellow rays
One by one charmed under each
Individual note

Your back as it bends
Lips over-ripe nectar
Lost in the cavern of your eyes
Breathing you as I would
Beyond death,
Where all that is left is love.

Harmony

It is her that makes the birds breed
The breeze blow

Flowers smile
Meadows speak

Her laughter rings songs
Tired ones
Love songs
Age old
Worn out scars of silence

Chirping harmonies
From a man
Becoming one voice

A compliment to all that is his missing piece
All that is her
An ode to her female

Strong, worn hands of the gentlest embrace
That build, mold
All that is their perfection

Forest

I long for your heart and mine is on fire
I'll carry your burdens with you
I'll shed my blood for you
You one day will let me
Understand the tyranny of my passion

Last time my love was in our upper body
You were unsure but you left
Smiling
On those lips, the ones that swallowed me whole

I grew and you didn't know
My words though let you in

Now, I'm surrounded by echoes of your silence
By sirens
By beats of drums

Many tempt me to touch their hair
To hold their breast in my chin
None though glide upon my solemn
Like your pastel covered posterior

Oh love me again!

Again, for souls like ours are meant for eternal unity

Garden of the Lovers Quarrel

From the tusks of the birch
An oriole flew
It's mouth taking with it my lover's chain
As the horn of the moon sat waiting to chime in dusk's anthem

I sat upon the marble chair when the earth spoke
Toward me my lover came, breasts wrapped in orange rinds and draped
in arms like ashes
Speaking the words of clouds falling under the sea of lunar waves

Hand in hand we walked to the stale pools
And thirsty were the dogs of death for their final laps of rotting leaves.
I traced my lover's thighs with the chalk of the morning, welcoming, but it
had forgotten our names.
We shared with it our blood and the harp from its mouth called us life's
sustenance

No More Stereo

It is your voice I miss
As it echoes the sky
Chanting, enchanting soft lips
Fairytale eyes
Pages of song dressing your skin
Resounding pollen sound - wind weaving your hair
Bouquets; divine crown

Here just broken syllables

Consort

In a fit of winter
She, to me, a cancer
Under my skin
The reflection
Me
In the same time
Alternate dimensions

Shapes through eyes of a wanderer
Spirit leaping bounds
Again this fever
To yet another destruction
For the joy of the rebuild

Tamed hardly
Just
On fire
The deepest burn
The origin
Flight

Puzzled
Pieces
Mine like the bitter bark
Woman sweet
Tempting
Not a play
Tired it succumbs

Time where this time does not bleed
Past the shadow
Inside the light
Eyes like beams
No face

Gnawing on fabric
Something simple
Essence
Absence unseen
But heard

Like bird to my bee
She is what is and what will be
Before creation
Until forever
Aside
Inside

Still

Not a sunrise,
Until it falls beyond the horizon,
Goes and not a minute more
That you do not tiptoe
Through my mind
Not on broken glass

Abandoned it is left
You pass through
And in my dreams
We stroke our
Soul with feathers
And skin with needles

The flowers in your hair
Are as fresh as the instant
They were picked
To this night
You become real again
A hallucination to my subconscious
But I feel you somehow
So how do we explain that?

A phantasm of pain
Like a lost appendage
In my red eyes
I omit any possibility of vain
And we fall so effortlessly
Again
Over and over

From Corners

And that it was
An evening glance from the corner of my eye
Your stare and
Turning I fell apart like
Houses of cards and toy block buildings

There I would have become your red carpet
Trumpets and confetti
In celebratory fashions

Instead I became an artist
Sculpting the rooms and writing like drunken poets
Fathering bourbon
Cheering to finest malts

Reflections on the midnight glass
Shuddering
Clinching my core
Vibrations like wild thunder

It was me there
A man with no words
From the corners of where the light enters
You a blur
More so than ever
The reoccurring dream
Plagued and in love

Petition

I beg for forgiveness
For the attention

To love,
Forgotten
Like a breeze come and gone
Felt but not seen

Appreciated
Now left standing
In the sun
No shade
Cover me! (pleading)

Not falling
Grasping
Final attempts
To not wait again
For a return

Love Abandoned

A sunrise again without your love
I see you still, closing my eyes
We dance and make love in dreams
Ride and play

At the end of each calendar day
When the light fades beyond the horizon
I long for slumber
For my unconsciousness
Last lingering bits of what remain of our bond that lie within

When the breeze touches your hair
Bird landing at your feet
The flower at your window
I am there
With love longing
Heart blistering

And when you call my name again
And in me you ignite that fire which kept us warm
Intensity surpassing what existed prior
I will answer in screams
To you I will sprint like love's finish line

For now I will miss you like the blues of the sky miss the clouds
And the peaks of the earth that touch them
Like the waves of the sea without shore to caress
And the rain that feeds them

The Poet's Plaudit to his Love (on love)

It is the sea
The effervescent tides
And you like fragile
On your coral boat
Of dreams

Lichen lace covered
Symbiosis
In your gentle smile
While moon comes
And goes

Songs of urchin
Between your toes

And his feathers
Fall
And with you
In love

Poem

In the drone of the unknown
The midnight quivers
Stars dance
Astrals call us to be

We as lovers sing
Chanting unison
Touching and revolving
Wobbling viciously on our axis

Fevered fellow poets awake
Painters wipe tears canvassing fingers
The dancer sprung in a fury of movement
Limitless it is

We call this glory

Little Rosa (the spirit in the black bird)

Bleeding out.
Every line.
Every letter.

Lower eyelids heavy.
Black birds bring gifts.
For every roach a stroke of terror.

Teeth grinding a mouth of dehydration.
Fists full of flesh.
Something that must be left behind.

Deserted in silence.
Not calm.
Screams never heard.
Not even by the screamer.

Bury me.
Oh bury me!

Malign

I am the dark in the hollow;
I'm the veins in the fallen leaves
You pick but I remain.

I am the putrid.
I am the cotton of your wool.

I,
the candle that ignites the many;
the soil that extinguishes.

The fumes, I am.
To your paint,
your solvent.

Burn, burn because I am.
That what was sought,
That of what is to come.

Swift Bird of Afterlife

If I were to drop from the tree at this moment
And if I do
May I, like flowers fall below the surface
After many years

Then creatures of the ground cycle through
My eyes, still orbs will
tumble from my voice
It says only things to the fibers below the roots
About how currently their veins thirst
While my teeth laugh in prejudice from lack of desire

No words will be cast
Once the caustic rain
Wears holes in my bones
And the wind tethers my skin in its whirls carrying it off to feed the city's
alleys

Remaining I will and be forgotten as casually as vivid dreams
But from my mind I will mold silver rings and aerate soil with my tongue
Walk hallways and whisper love from deaths ear
Light I will then bear to your flesh as heavily as fused iron

When flowers fall from trees and in those moments I inevitably join
My blood drained and corpse covered in nature's jewels
I will go beyond and leave my senses
And linger as I long unconfined
Leaving behind my disguise

Donde

Where does your body lie, poet?
It was in your last minutes/breath
In a cemetery
Bruised by soldiers
Clad were you by bullets?
Beaten?

Your songs sing still
In the child's mind
The dancing girl on southern side streets
They bring you flowers

The broken branch
You humble queer
Giving words to silent items
Duende pumping your veins

What you've become, in what you consumed yourself with - death.
A myriad now a lasting verse
Life's stanza

Love on shores of death's Mediterranean

Great poet where does your body lie?

76 Ride to Philly (for Mark Hannigan)

Here, come the sun
Its sound
Vibrations
On rails of the sky

Tempted photographs
Onward to a land of pilgrims
The cobblestones call
My name like the hoses
Delivering waste to my lungs

All the while two great ones slumber
I dance upon a page
Comfortable in the hands of the finale

Beckons he no more
For in a dream he came
Now a cube of granite
Remove him
To him from an oak barrel

As we glide toward the citrus
Toward the scales of the morning
We burn the trees

It may be another year 'for I see this again.

Poetics
of
Nature
and
Song

What I hear right now, no humanly venue could house. October rain upon leaves over dormant grass. Drops. Pressing the soil. And the chanting of the wind. There are no words that can mimic moments like these. No instrument that could play the tune.

Lament of Cornsilk's Salient

There was a great rising of the moon!
While I fell fast asleep, our closed eyes smiled.
And the stars brushed the night like cat faces.

With their cool covers they tried to calm that moon,
the one that breathed its drunken warm upon my dreams.

Outside I went and the questions I should have asked,
the actions one lets them become after being stirred,
were quiet eyes; locking eyes as vicious dogs.
Leading to a friendly submission.

I fought for slumber with the aid of your touch and my last thought of
that sky coming down so that I could fuel the ends of that arrow.
Wishing it would bond to those ivory lips like hot tar.

> Me
> Fighting back
> Leaving eternal scars.

I thought when the sun began its mid-summer ascent and my mind held
it like a warrior
> I the child hoping,
> the fury's end.

But the aggressive stare continued as the two fought like princes over-
throwing thrones.

The moon had its day and all of its fame!

Woodlawn

Have you ever graced yourself among the stones of the dead?
Caressed the paper bark of an old birch?
Kissed the shadows beyond the marble?
Peered through the iron gates to the furnace that burns bodies to ash?

Left they are in love and in honor
Saluting obelisks
Feeding century's old landscapes

Red foxes scurry after knowing revelations
Chapels crumble from neglect

And in this...
Something dealt with necessarily-
Brisk afternoons

Early April

The warm winds blew in spring
Pushing furiously
Ocean breezes to farm country

Late afternoon sky
Frictions percussing
Violent fury with midnight blues
Ferocious convictions from clouds lumbering voice

Plains hand themselves to the sky as if in love with its terror
Vulnerable but willing
A calm cool sets in
Gusts cease
As the silent calls the storm

A distant wall closing in
Falling liquid ringing
Sounds molding dust to mud
Earth's pheromones on humid strokes from upwinds

Shots ring and muzzle flashes
Snapshots of tree's blank stares
Cleansing

Siren

On the morning of the cool sun
I watched the seasons twist their
Miracles in hues

The scalp of the goddess sent me
Running through the trees
And I was the lonely bird calling
Down the drive

Calling to the Lord and to the Saints

"Make me your warrior!"

I rose like water in the tree of life.
Through every vein,
Out to every branch

Perma

On morrow
Dawn awakens slowly.
Result.
A hidden sun.

A step, in the air
        ... breathe.
Brisk and comforting among the quiet
Unlike the frigid.

Gently pressing the blanket of cold.
The trees appear ... lifeless.
World.
Dormant.
To eyes and glance.

Their secrets lie beyond.
This time.
Beyond vision,
Touch.

Look beyond
Through your eyes
Those of a poet.
Mine.
Ours.

Wind whispers fragments
Like us.
Fresh snow inviting
Luring.
It's not normal comfort.

A brief occurrence of a warm blooded.
Desperate for anything
And me.
Braided with time and nature.
Exhausting everything surrounding.

Absorbing
Beyond sight.
Kissing the beyond.
Embracing.
Inviting it back.
Back into words.

For those who long to see.

The Bay

A tender touch
Through the air
The sandy bottoms
And driftwood breeze spiral
Gliding its gentle hand down the coast

Gulls murmur sea songs
killdeer singing chorus of
Broken wings in semi-unison
An all too familiar song

Morning speaks with the rising sun
Their hush as the waves smile at the shore
Mussel shells still on dawn's decor

Buoys chime the act of man
Accompanies of steam ship horns
As nets are cast from commercial vessels
To feed the hungry

If it could be no other way the water snake accepts a magnified tan
Rainbow sliders dry on brittle branches piercing the water's edge

A lounge on grass at the edge of the dunes
An eternal calls the wandering home
Lost in whirlwinds of spirit and union
Bodies uniting

Softest Sand

Marine bodies; soils
Updrafts decay

Birds singing rebirth
Waves gliding fingers through muscle laden shores

A crane offered a seat
Beyond where the sand held home to areas of rest
Meditative trances
Manifested new beginnings

Pressed close to the heartbeat of Mother Earth
Through the palms of an archer
Words spoke through sealed lips

No steps were taken for granted
Returning to safe vessels
As air pushed upon his wings
The blue jay guided the way

Distracting; advocating peril

Coast

A tender touch
Through the air
The sandy bottoms
And driftwood breeze spiral
Gliding its gentle hand down the coast

Gulls murmur sea songs
killdeer singing chorus of
Broken wings in semi-unison
An all too familiar song

Morning speaks with the rising sun
Their hush as the waves smile at the shore
Mussel shells still on dawn's decor

Buoys chime the act of man
Accompanies of steam ship horns
As nets are cast from commercial vessels
To feed the hungry

If it could be no other way the water snake accepts a magnified tan
Rainbow sliders dry on brittle branches piercing the water's edge

A lounge on grass at the edge of the dunes
And eternal calls the wandering home
Lost in whirlwinds of spirit and union
Bodies uniting

Dire Melody

I don't want to hear music anymore.
Not the nails across the strings mocking the evening.
Nor the beat that easily pleases the searching soul.
The soul that devours.

I don't want to hear the singer's cries of wants.
So sorrowful in all of its joys.
Or the chime of hands like an audible wave after each conclusion.

I want the everlasting rhythm of the wind and the strum of it through the
trees.
To close my eyes to the sun's harp.

And feel.

The percussion of the skies.
The sea's siren.

Then we all dance in adolescence.
As Children of the earth.

Voice of Pleading Spring

So I feel the ghost
Of your embrace

You

Sun birthed love's constrictor

I

The tree who has forgotten
Broken from roots

Lounging in rivers
Drifting wood

Fear I have become if you are still

Maybe you are bits of composition,
Estranged banks
And the mouth of the river may be you,
Thrusting me-obliterations of memory
Toward far away foreign shores

But where my seeds hold tight
On these shores I will crumble

Song of Longing

Love, what are you?
Are you the birds mating in spring, falling from the trees?
You might be the fingers of wind's caress through a woman's hair.
The orange moon dragging its lips across midnight's inner thigh.

(Take me!)

I say to you Love,
Be me and my rising, like children on solstice.
Teach me your ways and make me glowing red.
Bend me on your anvil and plunge me into your cool solution.

(Take me!)

Break my morals as chalk under hammer and let the stars have me.
"Demands", you say.
They are but my nutrients.
You can burn my name in wood for your mantle.

(Take me!)

Not an evening passes where I do not make them wear your mask.
When I lay with spells cast upon the tired starving boy.
I wake in death's hour and cry for the morning and with it you.

(Take me!)

The blinding starbursts through the tears of my mistakes.
Beyond the phantoms of touch and the wind over your lips.
You find me and never worthy I bleed and you drink.

(Take me Love!)

Progression

The countless pigeons
With their two eyes
See vague slips of the tongue

The trees long to be the dew
Doing its best to perspire before
The sun pulls the sleep from its eyes
They cry tearless sobs – the closest
They will be to softening the soil

Then there are delicate creatures
That balance on saplings
Necks like underground spring waters
that meet the air
Mouths like spears that are thrust
Only because they must …be.

They are the brine whose chests
Lumber across the blue sky
Dying only from natural causes
And their acknowledgement of
Unnecessary sufferings
Witness that pour from their mouths;
Vines climbing upon the rocks.

Last.
Walks the poet who possesses nothing
He has lost everything
Flowing like carbon.
The current who goes unseen.
Taking with him empty hands.
Feeding them his blood.

Song of Crying River

Quiet river,
The city has lost you

Slowly passing

I hear you weep
Your lonely song

Slowly passing

While my tears fill you up they cannot wash away the sediments

Slowly passing

My gentle strokes for you,
only my long lost love
Mother of the lake

Slowly passing

Even the fish run from you and your desolate ways
But forever, I am your minnow

Slowly,
passing.

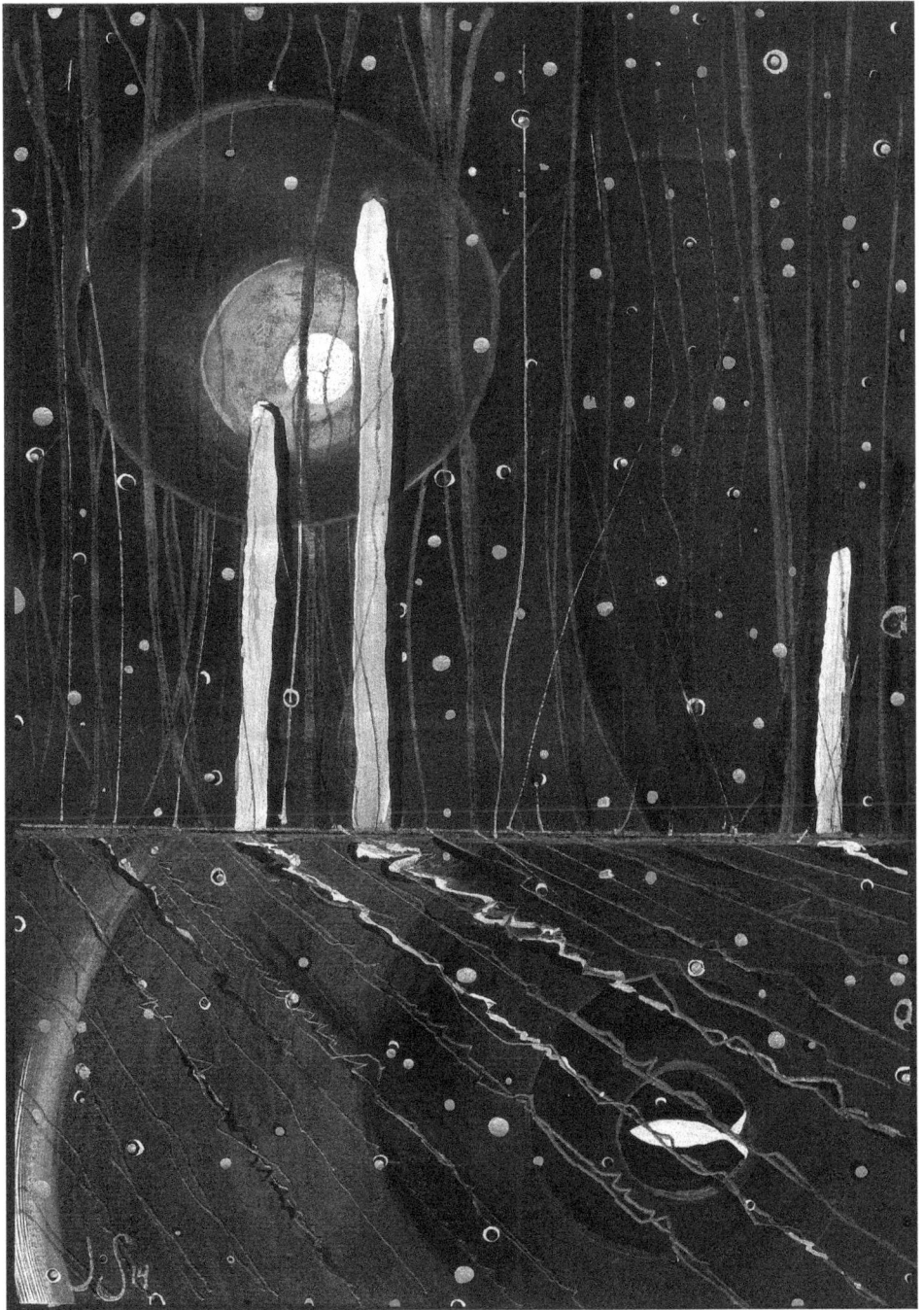

Thank You

… Special thank you to Mark and Kristina for getting my feet off the ground on this collection. The wings were moving they just needed a little breeze.
To my hero Michelle that cast the spell which manifested what you hold here in your hands.
To Jeff who spent hours upon hours, working, creating ...,
lovely Holly who put on the finishing touches.

Lastly to Northwest Ohio, my family, the living, the dead.

Kevin Fuller: kfullill@yahoo.com

Jeff Stewart (illustrations): jeffstewarttoledo@gmail.com

Holly K. Whitney (layout and jacket design): http://hollykwhitney.com

It was around 3:45 a.m. on the fifth of March. I awoke after setting myself on fire. I deemed once again my wonderful pieces of creativity could be left only to those who looked over my shoulder during their creation. As I watched the embers and charred slivers of their existence take flight in the early morning breeze I thought of self-immolation. How I remained still and silent in this sorrowful act watching the only pen still clipped to the spirals that held what was me together ... melt.

We turn pages so carelessly sometimes- the pages that hold the chapters to our lives. The words within that mean nothing. "What we invest in each other is all that remains." (M. Williams)

From the life of a poet transcending a life of a sinner I basked in its gentle warm glow. What could have never existed in the shed of my blood and in the time that held it within my body. Emergence now with mind and soul. Body left behind.

Then I awoke and now...

Silence.